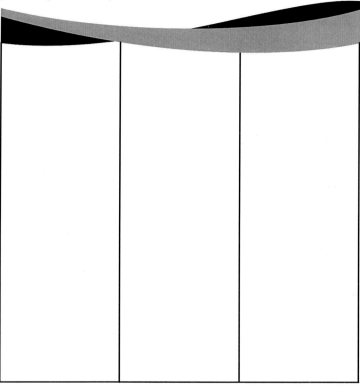

COMPUTERS

ADVENTURES IN
STEAM

Claudia Martin

WAYLAND
www.waylandbooks.co.uk

First published in Great Britain in 2017 by Wayland

Series editor: Izzi Howell
Designer: Rocket Design (East Anglia) Ltd
Illustrations: Rocket Design (East Anglia) Ltd
In-house editor: Julia Bird

ISBN: 978 1 5263 0473 5
10 9 8 7 6 5 4 3 2 1

MIX
Paper from
responsible sources
FSC® C104740

Wayland
An imprint of
Hachette Children's Group
Part of Hodder & Stoughton
Carmelite House
50 Victoria Embankment
London EC4Y 0DZ

An Hachette UK Company
www.hachette.co.uk
www.hachettechildrens.co.uk

Printed in China

Picture acknowledgements:
Alamy: Mark Scheuern 7b, IanDagnall Computing 22b, Interfoto 30t, ITAR-TASS Photo Agency 30b; Bcos47: 31t; ESO: 40t; Greg Hume: 18b; NASA/JPL: 41t; Shutterstock: SiiKA Photo 1, luskiv 3 and 29b, goodluz 4, 300 librarians 5, catshila 6, Everett Historical 7t and 23b, MO_SES Premium 9t, Syda Productions 9b, Titima Ongkantong 10, kiri11 11, pinkomelet 12, Parinya Suwannagood 13, Vitaly Korovin 14, MrGarry 15, Tatsianama 16t, Dmitry Kalinovsky 16b, Alexander Kirch 18t, Sudowoodo 19, Melody Smart 21, Tim Jenner 22t, Guy Erwood 23c, Oceans 24, Lifestyle Graphic 25t, Lifestyle Graphic 25b, dmitriylo 26, Denis Simonov 27t, N Azlin Sha 27b, MicroOne 28, Barone Firenze 29t, Bloomicon 31c, Peppinuzzo 31b, Ekaphon Maneechot 32, drserg 34, GLYPHstock 35, Wachiwit 36, Oleg Doroshin 38, Zoltan Kiraly 40b, Benny Marty 41b, Veselin Borishev 42, Vidoslava 43, Ahmet Misirligul 45; Sunzi99: 41c; US National Archives and Records Administration: 23t; US Navy photo by Chief Photographer's Mate Chris Desmond: 37.
Scratch is developed by the Lifelong Kindergarten Group at the MIT Media Lab. See http://scratch.mit.edu. The third party trademarks used in this book are the property of their respective owners, including the Scratch name and logo. The owners of these trademarks have not endorsed, authorised or sponsored this book.
All design elements from Shutterstock.

CONTENTS

A COMPUTER IS...

A COMPUTER IS A MACHINE CONTROLLED BY A SET OF INSTRUCTIONS CALLED .... A PROGRAM. MOST PEOPLE USE A COMPUTER EVERY DAY TO DO ALL SORTS OF THINGS, FROM HELPING WITH HOMEWORK TO LISTENING TO MUSIC.

Computers work with information, known as data. Computers are able to store data and carry out tasks with it, called processing. Then computers show the user the results of their work. Modern computers work with data in many different forms:

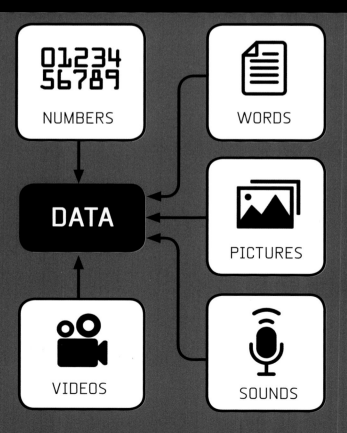

NUMBERS

WORDS

DATA

PICTURES

VIDEOS

SOUNDS

TECHNOLOGY TALK

A program is a list of instructions that tells a computer exactly what work to do. Without programs, a computer could not do anything at all. Programs are written by people called computer programmers, or 'coders'. Programs break down any task into its most basic steps, telling the computer what to do first, then next, then after that. Different programs do different jobs, such as sending emails or playing music.

SOFTWARE is all the programs that tell a computer what to do. Software is stored and runs on a computer's hardware.

HARDWARE is all the parts of a computer you can touch. When you look at the computer on your desk, the most obvious pieces of hardware are the screen and keyboard. However, many other bits of hardware are hidden away inside a computer.

Inside a computer, the motherboard holds crucial parts. One of these is the central processing unit (CPU), which carries out all the computer's calculations. There are also two types of memory, ROM and RAM (see page 14), for storing data and programs.

SCIENCE TALK

Today's computers are powered by electricity. A desktop computer is plugged into the mains electricity supply. Smartphones and laptops are powered by batteries, which can store a certain amount of electrical energy. They need recharging from the mains electricity supply. All computer data is carried in tiny flows of electricity called electric currents.

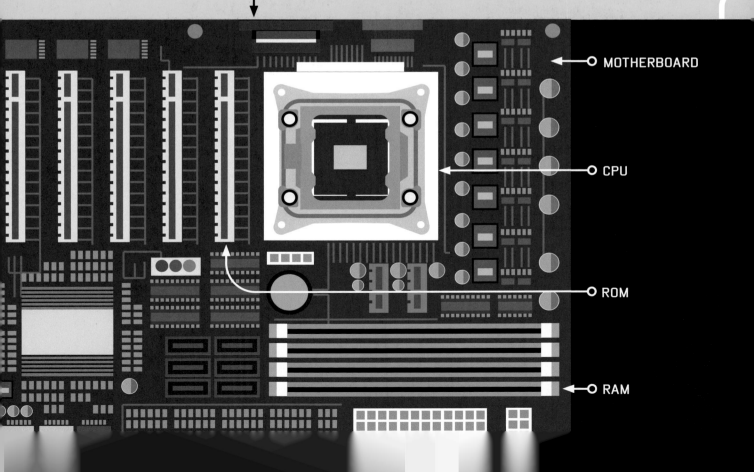

MOTHERBOARD

CPU

ROM

RAM

IN THE BEGINNING

THOUSANDS OF YEARS AGO, PEOPLE INVENTED CALCULATING DEVICES TO HELP THEM DO SUMS. THESE WERE NOT ELECTRONIC MACHINES, LIKE TODAY'S COMPUTERS, BUT THEY WERE THE FIRST STEP ON THE WAY. THE WORD 'COMPUTER' WAS FIRST USED IN 1613, DESCRIBING A PERSON WHO DID CALCULATIONS.

The abacus appeared over 4,000 years ago. Like modern computers, the abacus was a machine that performed operations by simplifying them. It was a step up from using stones or a tally chart to help with counting. The Chinese-style abacus has at least seven rods. In the upper section of each rod, there are two beads. In the lower section, there are five beads.

- On the first rod on the right, the upper beads represent 5s, while the lower beads represent 1s.

- On the second rod from the right, the upper beads represent 50s and the lower beads represent 10s.

- The values continue to increase by a factor of ten: to 100s, 1,000s and so on.

PROJECT

If you have an abacus, or can make a basic one using marbles or beads, try doing some addition and subtraction. Here is an example to get you started:

40 + 12 = 52

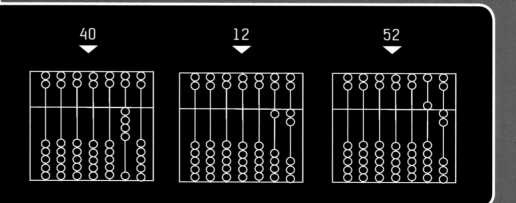

40   12   52

The first clockwork calculator was invented by the mathematician Blaise Pascal, in 1642. It was designed to help calculate how much tax people owed. It could add and subtract one number from another, by the turning of linked cogs. It did multiplication and division through repeated addition and subtraction. Sadly, the machine was too complicated to be very successful.

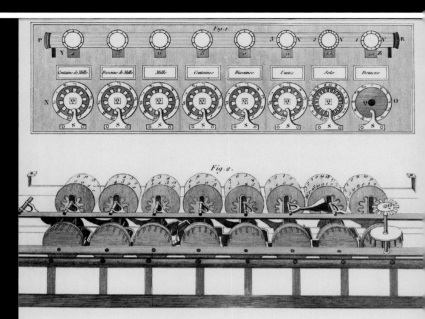

TECHNOLOGY TALK

A great step forward in the development of programmable machines was a loom invented by Joseph Marie Jacquard in 1801. Looms are machines that weave cloth. What was extraordinary about Jacquard's loom was that, for the first time, weavers could program the loom to weave a pattern. The program was in the form of punched cards, with holes representing the coloured threads making each pattern.

COMPUTERS EVERYWHERE

WHEN YOU THINK OF A COMPUTER, YOU PROBABLY IMAGINE A MACHINE WITH A SCREEN AND A KEYBOARD. THESE ARE CALLED PERSONAL COMPUTERS (PCS), BECAUSE THEY ARE FOR GENERAL USE BY ONE PERSON. BUT SOME COMPUTERS LOOK QUITE DIFFERENT...

There are several types of personal computers:

DESKTOP COMPUTERS These heavy computers are kept in one location. They have a separate screen and keyboard, and use a mouse as a pointing device for accessing locations on the screen. Most desktop computers also have a speaker, microphone and webcam.

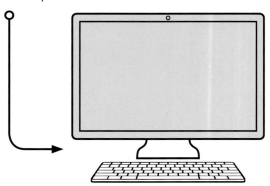

LAPTOPS These lightweight computers are usually in a 'clamshell' form, with a keyboard in the lower part of the 'shell' and a screen in the upper. Their pointing device is operated by touch, using a touchpad or trackpad.

SMARTPHONES As well as making voice calls and sending text messages, these mobile phones offer some of the same features as personal computers: they can access the web and run software.

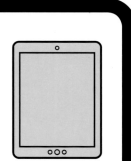

TABLETS Tablets are flat, hand-held devices. They are operated by touching the screen, called a touchscreen. Tablets have a camera, speaker and microphone, as well as an 'accelerometer', which monitors movement and makes sure the computer display is always upright.

There are 'hidden' computers everywhere. These computers are often programmed to perform a more limited set of tasks than personal computers. Most of them do not have a screen, keyboard or mouse, so you probably do not recognise them as computers at all. There are computers inside machines as varied as games consoles, cameras, cars, aeroplanes, traffic lights and robotic toys.

Just like your personal computer, the computer inside a cash machine works with data. That data includes your secret personal number, the amount of cash you want to withdraw and the total amount of money you have in your bank account. The computer's software gives instructions on how to use that data, then how to display the results of the work – usually by giving out cash.

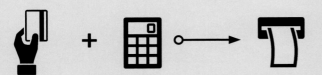

PROJECT

What tasks can you carry out on a personal computer? With an adult's help, try using a computer for these tasks over the next week. In each case, write down the name of the software you used to do it:

- Write a story.
- Draw a picture.
- Access a child-friendly website.
- Play a tune.
- Create a presentation. Why not display the results of your software research!

ONES AND ZEROS

A COMPUTER'S ELECTRICAL CIRCUITS CANNOT STORE AND PROCESS DATA IN THE FORM OF WORDS OR PICTURES. COMPUTERS TURN ALL THE DATA THEY RECEIVE INTO A FORM THEY CAN WORK WITH QUICKLY: NUMBERS.

Computers are digital devices. This means that they carry out all their operations using digits (numbers). Computers actually only work with two numbers: 0 and 1. These are known as the binary numbers.

MATHS TALK

In the binary number system, there are no numbers 2, 3, 4, 5, 6, 7, 8 and 9. Despite this, any number can be given in binary form. In binary, counting starts like this:

Binary value	Decimal value
0	0
1	1
1 0	2
1 1	3
1 0 0	4
1 0 1	5
1 1 0	6
1 1 1	7
1 0 0 0	8
1 0 0 1	9
1 0 1 0	10

Can you see the pattern? Now try counting from 11 to 20.

1 = On: electricity flowing

0 = Off: electricity stopped

Binary numbers turn a computer's electrical circuits on and off. The CPU contains many tiny circuits with switches in them. Like a light switch, these mini switches turn the flow of electricity in the circuit on or off. A 1 turns the electricity on. A 0 turns it off. The constant turning on and off of electrical circuits is what allows a computer to carry out its work.

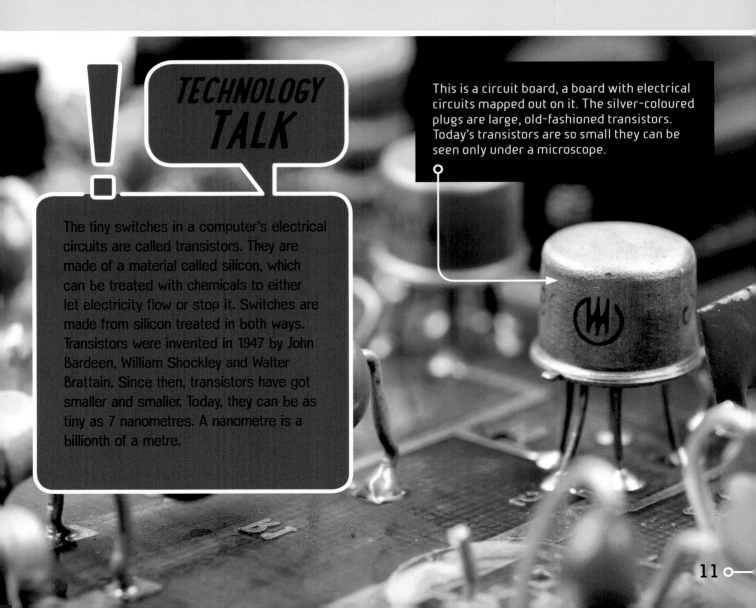

TECHNOLOGY TALK

The tiny switches in a computer's electrical circuits are called transistors. They are made of a material called silicon, which can be treated with chemicals to either let electricity flow or stop it. Switches are made from silicon treated in both ways. Transistors were invented in 1947 by John Bardeen, William Shockley and Walter Brattain. Since then, transistors have got smaller and smaller. Today, they can be as tiny as 7 nanometres. A nanometre is a billionth of a metre.

This is a circuit board, a board with electrical circuits mapped out on it. The silver-coloured plugs are large, old-fashioned transistors. Today's transistors are so small they can be seen only under a microscope.

A COMPUTER'S BRAIN

THE CPU IS A KEY PIECE OF HARDWARE. IT CARRIES OUT ALL THE COMPUTER'S CALCULATIONS AND CONTROLS ITS OTHER HARDWARE.

To carry out any task, every computer follows the same process:

○ **INPUT** The computer receives data. This is known as input.

○ **MEMORY** When a computer receives input, the CPU and the memory work hand in hand: the CPU reads programs stored in the memory, and stores data in the memory.

○ **PROCESSING** The computer processes the data in its CPU.

○ **OUTPUT** The computer gives the user the results of its work. This is known as output.

THINKING OUTSIDE THE BOX!

You can think of your brain as your own CPU. Consider how you do a calculation:

1 You receive the instruction from your teacher to add 1 + 2.

2 You search your memory for the method of how to do addition.

3 You use your brain to work out the sum.

4 You give your result (which is 3!) by writing it down or telling your teacher.

1 INPUT

2 MEMORY

3 PROCESSING

4 OUTPUT

Modern CPUs are small, flat 'chips' of silicon called microprocessors. They are also called 'integrated circuits'. Microprocessors contain billions of tiny circuits with switches that can be turned on or off. Before microprocessors were invented in 1971, computers were very bulky because they were built from racks of circuit boards containing many different circuits (see page 23).

MATHS TALK

The more switches, or transistors, a CPU has, the faster it can process data. In 1975, the electronics expert Gordon Moore predicted that computer processing power would double every two years. He was right! That is because we have learnt how to make tinier and tinier transistors and pack them onto microprocessors. Today's most powerful microprocessor contains 7.2 billion transistors. However, will the increase in processing power continue? Some people think that transistors are now as small as they possibly can be.

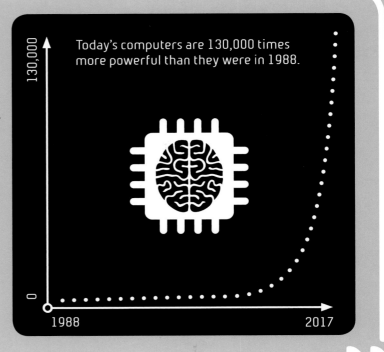

Today's computers are 130,000 times more powerful than they were in 1988.

130,000

1988   2017

MEMORY

TWO IMPORTANT PARTS OF
A COMPUTER'S MEMORY ARE
FOUND ON ITS MOTHERBOARD:
THE ROM AND THE RAM. A USER
CAN ALSO SAVE INFORMATION TO
A COMPUTER'S HARD DISK OR BY
PLUGGING IN AN EXTERNAL
MEMORY DEVICE.

Hard disks save data onto a spinning disk.
When the data is needed again, the moving arm
goes straight to the correct area of the disk.

ROM
The 'read only memory'
stores programs and data even
when the computer is off. The
computer's user cannot save
anything to the ROM.

RAM
The 'random access memory' is
where data is stored while the
user is working. When the user
turns off the computer, the data is
lost – unless it is saved to the hard
disk first!

HARD DISK
Hard disks are found in desktop
computers, but some tablets use
memory chips instead. The hard
disk is where the user can store
programs and files. Files are blocks
of data, such as a letter or a photo.

" MATHS TALK

In 1956, the first hard disk weighed 1,000 kg
and was the size of two refrigerators. It stored
only 3.75 megabytes of data. Today's most
powerful hard disks weigh 62 g, the weight
of an egg, and hold 10 terabytes of data (see
Maths Talk opposite).

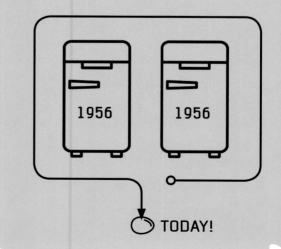

1956   1956

TODAY!

If you need more memory space, you can save data onto external memory devices. It is also good practice to back up (make copies of) files on an external device in case your computer breaks.

MEMORY STICK
Memory sticks (also known as flash drives or USB sticks), which fit in a pocket, are useful for carrying data from one computer to another.

MEMORY DEVICES

MEMORY CARD
Memory cards can be slipped into laptops, tablets and smartphones.

CLOUD STORAGE
Cloud storage is when data is saved onto computers somewhere else in the world, usually in a data centre. Data is sent over the Internet (see pages 32–33).

MATHS TALK

Like distance is measured in centimetres, metres and kilometres, memory is measured in bytes, kilobytes, megabytes, gigabytes and terabytes. One byte holds 8 binary digits. A kilobyte holds 8,000 binary digits. A terabyte holds 8 trillion binary digits. A file containing 100 words of text might be around 45 kilobytes, while a photo taken by a digital camera is 1 megabyte or more.

⇥ INPUTS

YOU ARE PROBABLY FAMILIAR WITH USING INPUT DEVICES SUCH AS KEYBOARDS, MICE AND TOUCHSCREENS. THERE ARE ALSO MANY OTHER DEVICES AND SENSORS THAT CAN GIVE A COMPUTER INFORMATION.

KEYBOARDS On a computer keyboard, each key is a switch that sends an electronic signal to the computer. The computer's software is able to interpret the different key presses.

SCANNERS Scanners are used to capture images of photos or paper documents placed in the machine. A colour scanner registers how much red, green and blue (the primary colours) are in each tiny portion of the image. The scanner then converts this information into digital form.

MICE Usually, mice shine a bright light onto your desk, some of which reflects back off the desk into a sensor. As the mouse moves, the pattern of reflected light changes. The mouse converts these patterns into electronic signals.

BARCODE READERS These input devices read the barcodes that label goods. Barcodes are patterns of black and white lines that represent numbers. A light sensor shines a beam of light on the barcode and measures the reflected light. Black reflects less light than white. The reader translates the pattern into binary digits: black is 0, and white is 1.

0 10421 25071 3

THINKING OUTSIDE THE BOX!

Mice do their job so well that most people never think about alternatives. However, there are other hand-held pointing devices, which are not so widely used. One is a stylus, a pen-shaped device used with touchscreens. Another is a light pen, which shines light onto a special computer screen. Can you think of a new design for a hand-held input?

Some computers accept inputs that are spoken. To accept voice inputs, a computer needs a microphone and speech recognition software. When we speak, our words have patterns of loud and soft sounds. For example, a hard consonant, like a p, is a sudden, loud sound. Voice recognition software compares the patterns of loud and soft with the 50 or so phonemes (speech sounds) in its database.

TECHNOLOGY TALK

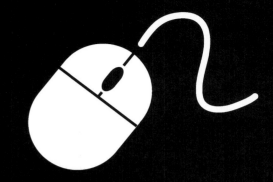

Smartphones and tablets have touchscreens, while laptops have trackpads in place of a mouse. A grid of electrical circuits lies beneath the touchscreen or trackpad. These pick up the movement of your fingers and send electrical signals to the computer. Many touchscreens can recognise particular touches, such as pinches to zoom in, and swipes to turn the pages of an ebook.

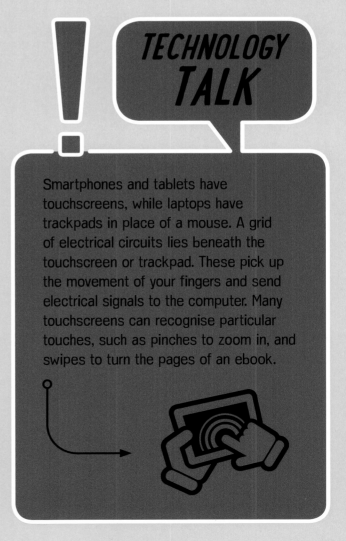

OUTPUTS

WHEN YOU TYPE WORDS INTO A COMPUTER, THE COMPUTER USUALLY SHOWS THEM ON ITS SCREEN. IT CAN ALSO SEND THEM TO A PRINTER, OR IT CAN BROADCAST THEM THROUGH A SPEAKER. THESE ARE ALL OUTPUT DEVICES.

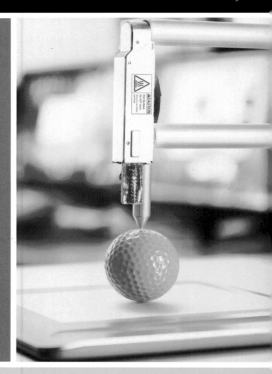

Today, computer screens are usually liquid crystal displays (LCDs). LCDs are covered in thousands of pixels, or tiny areas of the screen. Each pixel has three sub-pixels: red, green and blue. When an electronic signal containing data (such as words, a picture or a video) is sent to a pixel, the liquid crystal changes to allow light to shine through. Depending on the colour the pixel needs to show, it allows light to shine through the red, green and blue sub-pixels in different amounts. Any colour can be created by combining those three primary colours.

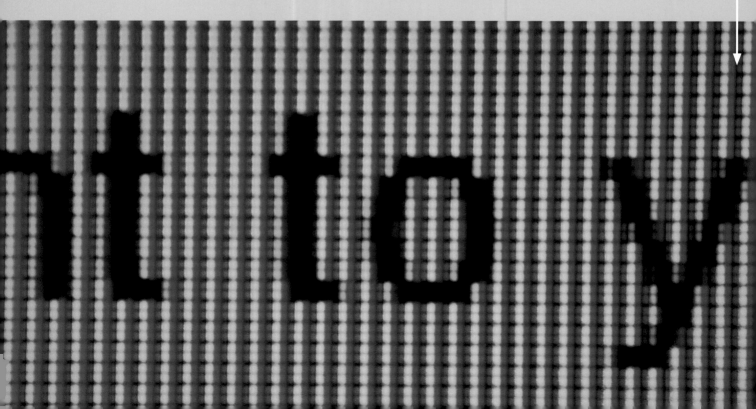

THINKING OUTSIDE THE BOX!

If you look back at the 'hidden' computers on page 9, you might be able to think of more output devices for computers. For example, the computer in a traffic light is programmed to change the colour displayed by its lights in a sequence. The lights are its output device. What do you think are the output devices for a talking robot?

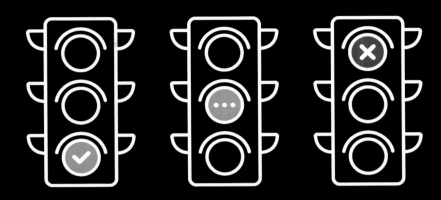

A computer sends data to a printer as electrical signals through wires, or as radio waves through the air. The printer converts the signals into their final form: a black and white document, a colour photo or even a three-dimensional (3D) object. 3D printers create an object layer by layer, using plastic or metal.

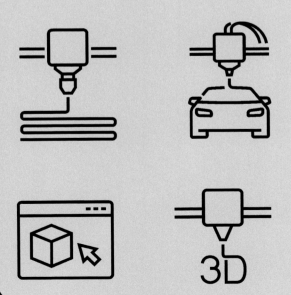

TECHNOLOGY TALK

Another common computer output is sound, such as speech, game sound effects or music. Sound travels through the air as vibrations. These vibrations are picked up by a computer's microphone, which turns them into electrical signals. A computer's sound card converts these signals into binary numbers. Many computer programs can be used to edit sounds. To output, the sounds are turned back into electrical signals and sent to a computer's speaker. The signals make the speaker's cone vibrate, creating sounds.

PROGRAMMING

A PROGRAM IS AN ORDERED SET OF INSTRUCTIONS. COMPUTER PROGRAMMERS WRITE THEIR INSTRUCTIONS IN ONE OF MANY PROGRAMMING LANGUAGES, OFTEN CALLED CODE.

First, a programmer decides exactly what the computer needs to do, then breaks down the instructions into step-by-step commands that cannot be misunderstood. Rather than typing the same command over and over, programmers often create subroutines. These are parts of a program that need to be repeated. For example, every time the programmer wants to command the computer to play a tune, they tell the computer to run the 'play a tune' subroutine. Sometimes even experienced programmers make a mistake though! A bug is any mistake that stops a program from working, like saying 'Turn left' when you mean 'Turn right'.

PROJECT

Write a program that commands a friend to walk around the playground:

- Choose a pattern for your friend to walk in, perhaps a square or hexagon shape.

- Break down your instructions into easy-to-understand commands, such as number of steps forward, and quarter or half turns.

- Do you want to include any subroutines?

- Now insert a bug into your program, without causing your friend an injury!

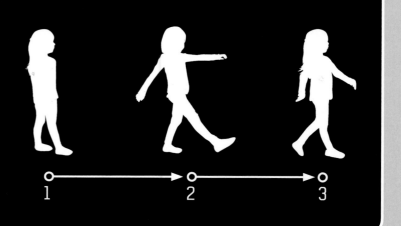

COMPUTER PROGRAMS.

Different programming codes or languages are written in collections of numbers, symbols or words. Whatever the programming language, a computer's 'interpreter' program converts it into strings of 1s and 0s. The computer languages you may use in school include Scratch, Logo, Java and Python.

PROJECT

With an adult's permission, try out Scratch. In Scratch, it is easy to program a sprite to move around the screen. A sprite does what you say, like your friend in the playground. The standard Scratch sprite is a cat. You give it instructions in the form of coloured blocks with commands written on them, such as 'Move 10 steps'.

- Go to https://scratch.mit.edu/ and click 'Try it out'.

- Find the blocks that command the cat sprite to move. They are in the dark blue Motion group, in the centre of the screen. Drag some of those blocks over to the empty area on the right side of the screen.

- Click on the blocks to see what the sprite does.

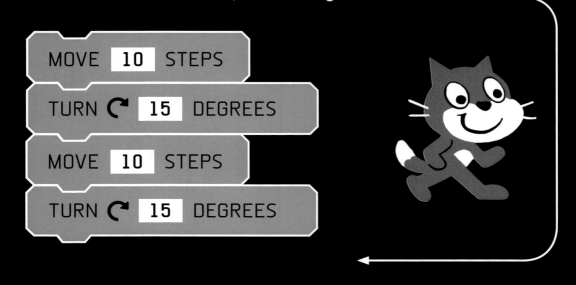

HALL OF FAME: COMPUTER SCIENTISTS

THE TECHNOLOGY IN YOUR LAPTOP OR SMARTPHONE WAS DEVELOPED STEP BY STEP OVER MANY DECADES. SOME GREAT THINKERS AND INVENTORS PLAYED A ROLE IN THAT JOURNEY.

CHARLES BABBAGE (1791–1871)

The English mathematician Charles Babbage is often called the 'father of computing'. In 1837, he designed the earliest true computer, the Analytical Engine, although he only built part of it. It was to be the first programmable calculating machine, using punched cards, based on those invented by Joseph Marie Jacquard (see page 7). Any calculation could be carried out by a system of interlocking gears. The machine was to be powered by steam.

ADA LOVELACE (1815–1852)

Ada Lovelace, daughter of the English poet Lord Byron, was a friend of Babbage's. A talented mathematician, she saw the potential of the (unbuilt) Analytical Engine to be more than just a calculator. She wrote the first ever algorithm (a way of solving problems in a series of steps) to be used by the Engine. This made her the world's first computer programmer.

HERMAN HOLLERITH (1860-1929)

US inventor Herman Hollerith invented the punched-card tabulator, an electrical machine that recorded and sorted information. This was a breakthrough in data processing. The idea was that any piece of information could be recorded by a hole punched in a card. If a particular area on the card represented gender, for example, a hole there could mean 'male'. The system was initially used for recording information about the population for the United States Census Office.

ALAN TURING (1912-1954)

The English scientist Alan Turing developed many of our ideas about how computers might work, although his 1936 'Turing machine' was only a very complex idea, not a real machine. In particular, he studied how a future electronic computer might be controlled by strings of binary numbers. He predicted that computers would one day be able to think like humans, which we call artificial intelligence. Today, Turing is also remembered for being persecuted for being gay.

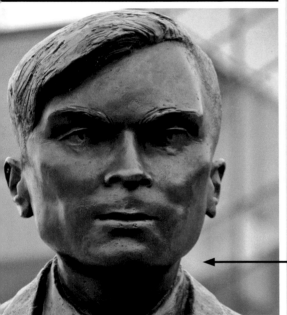

JOHN MAUCHLY (1907-1980) AND J. PRESPER ECHERT (1919-1995)

These US inventors built the first general-purpose electronic digital computer, called ENIAC (Electronic Numerical Integrator and Calculator), in 1946. Its input, output and memory storage were in the form of punched cards. It could multiply two 10-digit numbers 357 times in a second. ENIAC took up 167 square metres of floor space and weighed 30 tons!

SOFTWARE

WHEN YOU USE YOUR COMPUTER, ONE SORT OF SOFTWARE ALLOWS YOU TO DRAW PICTURES, ANOTHER LETS YOU SEND EMAILS OVER THE INTERNET, WHILE YET ANOTHER LETS YOU SURF THE WEB.

A key piece of software is a computer's operating system. This controls the computer's basic functions and how other software uses the CPU and memory. It interprets inputs, turning them into 1s and 0s. Microsoft Windows is the most common operating system for desktop computers. Many mobile devices, such as tablets and smartphones, run the Android operating system. However, Apple Macintosh desktop computers run the Mac OS operating system, and Apple mobile devices run iOS.

ART TALK

Modern operating systems communicate with the user through a graphical user interface (GUI). They were first developed in the early 1980s. A GUI is the system of drop-down menus, docks and icons that you click on to tell the computer to perform different tasks. We tend to take GUIs for granted, but look more closely to see how cleverly designed they are. Many functions are shown in pictures rather than words. Today, children learn to use and understand GUIs in much the same way they learn to read.

Examine the GUI on your personal computer. Would you change its design if you could, or does it already work perfectly?

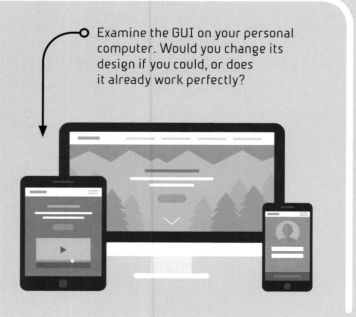

HOUSEHOLD SOFTWARE

The software on your home computer may include a word-processing program for typing documents, an email program, a web browser for reading websites, and media players for playing music and videos. Anti-virus software prevents your computer being damaged by dangerous software, called viruses, that travel from computer to computer over the Internet.

PROFESSIONAL SOFTWARE

Many programs were created to help people perform their jobs more easily. These include programs for creating presentations or spreadsheets, design programs in 2D or 3D, website design programs, and programs for creating animations.

TECHNOLOGY TALK

Software is designed for a particular purpose and a particular 'platform', meaning the type of computer or operating system. For example, some software is designed specially for mobile devices such as smartphones and tablets. These programs are called apps, short for applications. The first app store, selling apps online, opened in 2008. One very successful app is the game *Candy Crush Saga*, which has been downloaded over 500 million times.

GRAPHICS

THE EARLIEST PERSONAL COMPUTERS COULD DISPLAY ONLY ONE-COLOUR TEXT AND NUMBERS. DEVELOPMENTS IN COMPUTERS HAVE LED TO MORE REALISTIC AND EXCITING GRAPHICS.

By the 1980s, personal computers were beginning to have full-colour screens. By the 1990s, faster processing speeds were making graphics quicker to create. Alongside these developments came changes in photography, with photos stored on computers rather than film. Today, software developers have written many programs for creating graphics and editing photos. There are two main types of graphics:

In this 1980s bitmap graphic, it is possible to see the separate pixels.

BITMAP GRAPHICS Pictures are made up of pixels of different colours. Many artworks are bitmaps, as well as photographs taken on a digital camera.

VECTOR GRAPHICS Pictures are made up of lines and shapes. Vectors can be enlarged without the separate pixels becoming visible. Logos are often created using vector graphics.

PROJECT

Try out a bitmap graphics program. If you're using a Windows desktop computer, try the free program Microsoft Paint. On a Mac, try Paint X Lite.

- Create a pattern using squares and circles of different sizes. To do this, you will need to find the 'Rectangle' and 'Ellipse' tools.

- Find the 'Fill' tool, then fill the shapes with different colours by clicking in them. Now print out your design.

RECTANGLE TOOL   ELLIPSE TOOL   FILL TOOL

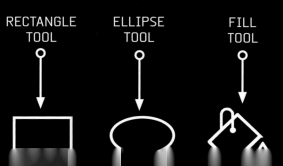

The term computer-generated imagery (CGI) is used to describe the 3D graphics created for video games, films and TV shows. Outside the world of entertainment, CGI is also employed by architects and engineers to design structures. To create a CGI character or building, the artist builds it from a mesh of lines. A surface, colour and texture are added to the mesh. Then the character or building can be manipulated and seen from different angles, without redrawing it. CGI is created using a combination of bitmaps and vectors.

CGI can make extinct creatures, giant armies and alien planets look real!

THINKING OUTSIDE THE BOX!

In the early 1990s, animators at the company Pixar wanted to make a film entirely using CGI. This had never been done before. The problem was that CGI was not yet so advanced that it could show the range of facial expressions and movements that make humans appear human. To solve the problem, the film-makers had a great idea: to make a children's film with toys as the characters. The result was *Toy Story*, released in 1995.

GAMES

COMPUTER GAMES HAVE BECOME INCREASINGLY REALISTIC, WITH FAST-MOVING GRAPHICS AND ATMOSPHERIC SOUND EFFECTS. GAMES CAN BE PLAYED ON A RANGE OF PLATFORMS, FROM GAMES CONSOLES TO SMARTPHONES.

Computer games first became popular in the 1970s. They were usually played on coin-operated machines in arcades. An arcade machine has a video game computer, a screen, speakers and a game controller, in the form of a joystick, wheel or buttons. A games console is a computer specially made for playing games. They can be hand-held devices with a built-in screen. Home games consoles are larger and are usually connected to a television screen. Although consoles first appeared in 1966, it was at least another decade before they became widespread. An early popular console was the hand-held Game Boy®, released in 1989.

Across the world, the video game industry makes around £90 billion every year. At present, more than half this money is earned from sales of games consoles and their games. Games bought for playing on personal computers earn about a quarter of the money. Games played on smartphones make more than £20 million every year, and they are getting more popular.

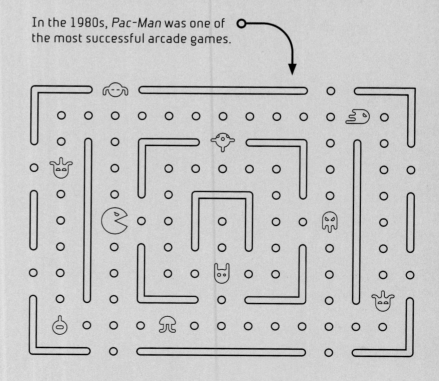

In the 1980s, *Pac-Man* was one of the most successful arcade games.

Most home games consoles have hand-held controllers as input devices, with buttons or joysticks for controlling movement in the game. Some game controllers, such as the Wii remote, contain motion sensors. Another common input device is a touch-sensitive mat for use in dancing games. With some consoles, the player does not have to touch an input device at all. For example, the Xbox 360 uses a Kinect camera to detect the player's movements.

The Kinect input device responds to motion and spoken commands.

" ART TALK

Many popular games offer virtual worlds, where players can interact with other players. The player chooses an avatar, a sprite that represents them in the world. Often the avatar can be designed by the player to look like themself, or to be strange and surprising. In an ordinary game, the graphic backgrounds may be realistic or beautiful, but in a virtual world they are designed as a key part of the player's enjoyment and interaction with the game. Popular virtual worlds include *Minecraft* and *Second Life*.

In *Minecraft*, a player can design their own houses, parks and cities.

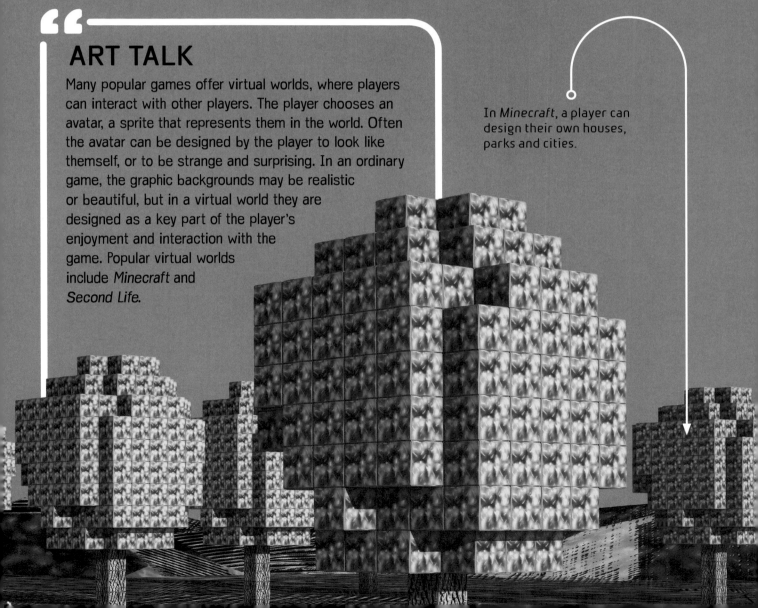

HALL OF FAME: PERSONAL COMPUTERS

THE EARLIEST COMPUTERS FILLED A WHOLE ROOM. AS A RESULT, THEY COULD BE USED ONLY BY GOVERNMENTS AND LARGE ORGANISATIONS. A SERIES OF BREAKTHROUGHS LED TO THE DEVELOPMENT OF TODAY'S PERSONAL COMPUTERS, WHICH ARE FOUND IN OFFICES, HOMES AND POCKETS.

APPLE II, 1977

This was one of the first ready-to-use personal computers with a microprocessor. It was designed by Steve Wozniak and Steve Jobs, co-founders of the Apple computer company. The Apple II was initially sold for US$1,298, which is equivalent to about £4,000 in today's money.

MOUSE, 1963

The mouse was invented by US computer engineers Douglas Engelbart and William English in 1963. The first mouse had a wooden shell, a circuit board and two metal wheels. Nine years later, English developed the design by replacing the wheels with a ball that could monitor movement in any direction. In 1973, the Xerox Alto was the first desktop computer to be used with a mouse.

SMARTPHONE, 1994

In 1994, the IBM Simon was the first mobile phone to also run software, and had a touchscreen used with a stylus. Applications included an address book, calendar, calculator, clock and electronic note pad. Simon could also send and receive emails. It was three years later, in 1997, that the first smartphones were given web browsers for searching the web.

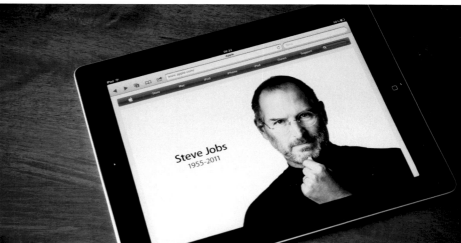

IPAD, 2010

Tablet-style computers have been available since the early years of the 21st century, but they did not become truly popular until Apple launched the iPad in 2010. The iPad's success is due to its many built-in functions, such as wireless Internet connection, camera and music library.

GOOGLE GLASS, 2013

This wearable computer featured a screen and camera. It accepted inputs from voice commands and a touchpad on the side. Google Glass was withdrawn from sale after a year, partly because people were worried about being secretly filmed. However, the future of computing may still lie in wearable devices.

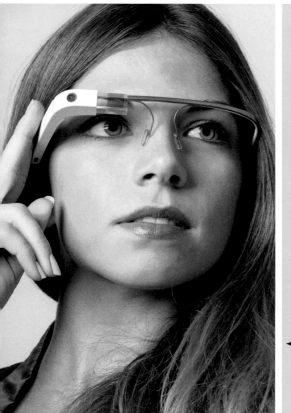

NETWORKS

THE EARLIEST NETWORKS USED WIRES TO CONNECT THE COMPUTERS IN A BUILDING. TODAY, THE INTERNET IS A VAST COMPUTER NETWORK COVERING THE WHOLE WORLD.

Networks are a way of sharing data and other resources. Wired networks are created by copper wires or optical fibres. Many homes are connected by copper wires, along which data is sent as electrical signals. Most new networks use optical fibres, along which data travels as pulses of light. Optical fibre networks carry data much faster than copper wire.

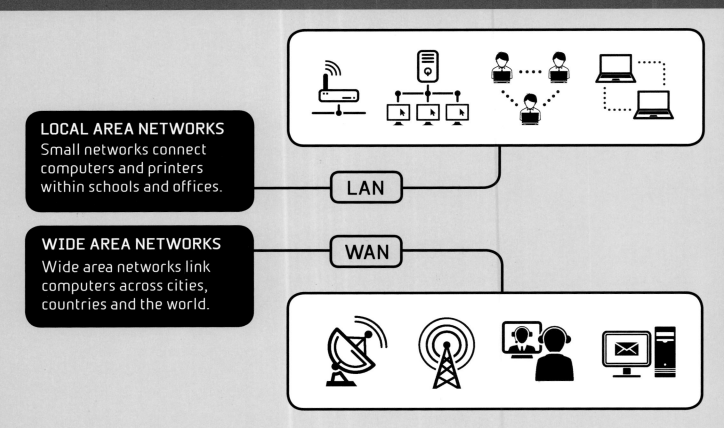

LOCAL AREA NETWORKS
Small networks connect computers and printers within schools and offices.

LAN

WIDE AREA NETWORKS
Wide area networks link computers across cities, countries and the world.

WAN

TECHNOLOGY *TALK*

In a wireless network, data is usually sent and received using radio waves. On a global scale, communications satellites orbiting the Earth receive and transmit data wirelessly. On a smaller scale, wireless local area networks often use a system called Wi-Fi. A Wi-Fi network covers a single home or business. A device called a wireless router sends and receives radio waves within the building. The router is often connected to a larger network, either wired or wireless.

People often use the words 'web' and 'Internet' as if they mean the same thing. In fact, the Internet is a worldwide network, made up of thousands of kilometres of cables as well as wireless connections. Like all networks, the Internet is a way of exchanging data, and it is commonly used for sending and receiving emails. It is also used for accessing millions of websites: the 'web'.

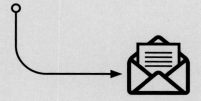

MATHS TALK

The word 'Internet' was first used in 1974, when local networks started to merge into one giant network. Then, there were just a few hundred people connected to the Internet. Today, more than 3.4 billion people are connected to it.

• The country with the highest percentage of Internet users is Iceland, with 100 per cent of its population having Internet access.

• The country with the lowest proportion is Eritrea in East Africa, where only 1 per cent have Internet access.

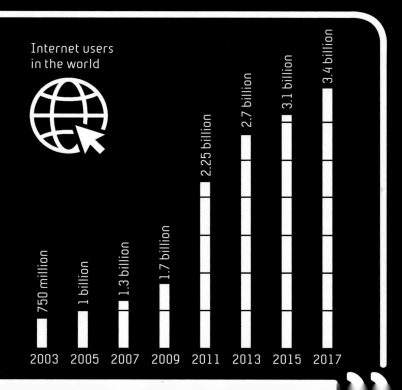

Internet users in the world

2003	750 million
2005	1 billion
2007	1.3 billion
2009	1.7 billion
2011	2.25 billion
2013	2.7 billion
2015	3.1 billion
2017	3.4 billion

THE WEB

WHENEVER WE LOOK AT A WEBSITE, WE ARE USING THE WORLD WIDE WEB. WEBSITES ALLOW US TO FIND OUT THE NEWS, WATCH VIDEOS, BUY CLOTHES, PLAY GAMES AND LINK UP WITH FRIENDS.

A website is a document stored on a computer somewhere in the world. These documents can contain words, images and videos. Websites are written in a special computer language called Hypertext Mark-up Language (HTML). Websites and webpages are connected by hyperlinks: when we click on a link, we move from one webpage to another.

The web was invented by English computer scientist Tim Berners-Lee in 1989.

TECHNOLOGY TALK

We view websites using software called a web browser. Google Chrome and Internet Explorer are popular browsers. When we type the address of a website into our browser, the browser sends a request over the Internet: it asks the computer storing the website to send it to our computer. The data is returned via the Internet. The browser then follows the instructions in the HTML to display the website on our computer.

Web addresses are like postal addresses: they are a way of identifying a particular website. All web addresses start with the letters 'http', which stands for Hypertext Transport Protocol: the set of rules that govern how websites are transported over the Internet. Most websites then have the letters 'www', which stand for World Wide Web. The end of a web address, called its suffix, can tell us something about the organisation that runs the website, for example:

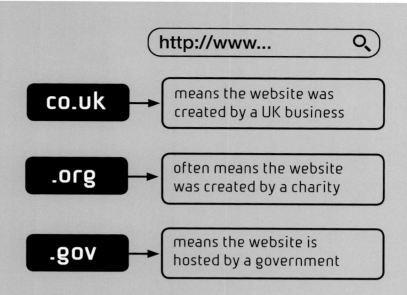

co.uk → means the website was created by a UK business

.org → often means the website was created by a charity

.gov → means the website is hosted by a government

THINKING OUTSIDE THE BOX!

The World Wide Web opens up huge possibilities for knowledge and communication. However, when we are using the web, it is important to think about how we do it. Anyone can create a website containing information that is false or harmful. When we use websites that allow us to communicate directly with other people, often called social networking, we need to think about how we behave and to watch out for how others behave. Since the web is created by people, it can only be as good or as bad as the people who use it.

VIRTUAL REALITY

VIRTUAL MEANS 'ALMOST'. VIRTUAL REALITY IS WHEN A COMPUTER CREATES A WORLD THAT APPEARS TO BE RIGHT IN FRONT OF YOU, BUT IT IS REALLY ONLY THE PRODUCT OF A PROGRAM.

Rather than viewing virtual reality on a screen, it is viewed through a headset. In gaming, virtual reality headsets allow the player to feel as if they are completely in the world of the game. Motion sensors in the headset pick up on head movements and the program changes the view to match the movements. Virtual reality gloves and body suits give the feeling of touching something in the virtual world by applying slight pressure to the skin.

ART TALK

Augmented reality (AR) can be found in software for mobile computer devices, such as smartphones and tablets. Augmented reality is different from virtual reality: it offers a view of the real world through the device's camera, with added features, such as useful or entertaining graphics, sounds or text. The game *Pokémon Go*, released in 2016, features virtual creatures who appear on screen as if in the real world. Players must locate them. A drawback of augmented reality is that users can be distracted from taking care in the real world! In 2016, two men playing *Pokémon Go* walked off a cliff. Luckily, they were not badly hurt.

Although virtual reality is most commonly used in games, it is also used in some workplaces. Its technology can be helpful for training soldiers, who experience the feeling of being in battle without putting themselves at risk. Surgeons are also able to train using virtual reality, giving them a lifelike experience of performing surgery without the need for a human body.

This soldier is learning how to make a parachute jump using a virtual reality program.

THINKING OUTSIDE THE BOX!

Can you think of other jobs or activities for which virtual reality would be useful? What about situations where augmented reality could offer helpful features? Consider the worlds of education, construction, shopping, transport and government.

ARTIFICIAL INTELLIGENCE

AT PRESENT, MOST PERSONAL COMPUTERS ONLY DO EXACTLY WHAT WE TELL THEM. HOWEVER, SOME COMPUTERS ARE PROGRAMMED TO 'THINK FOR THEMSELVES', LIKE A HUMAN DOES. THESE COMPUTERS ARE SAID TO HAVE ARTIFICIAL INTELLIGENCE.

Computers just do whatever they are told by their programs. AI itself is created by programming. AI programs use mathematical algorithms to allow a computer to decide between different responses to a question. These programs also allow the computer to 'learn' from past events. This is accomplished through algorithms: if action A produces this result, but action B produces a better result, in future action B will be chosen.

THINKING OUTSIDE THE BOX!

Computers and robots with AI have featured in fiction since 1920, when the Czech writer Karel Čapek wrote a play about robots rebelling against their human masters. Countless other books, films and TV shows have focussed on the dangers of computers thinking for themselves, including the 2004 film *I, Robot* and the 2015 children's TV show *Eve*. Why do you think humans are both fascinated and worried by AI?

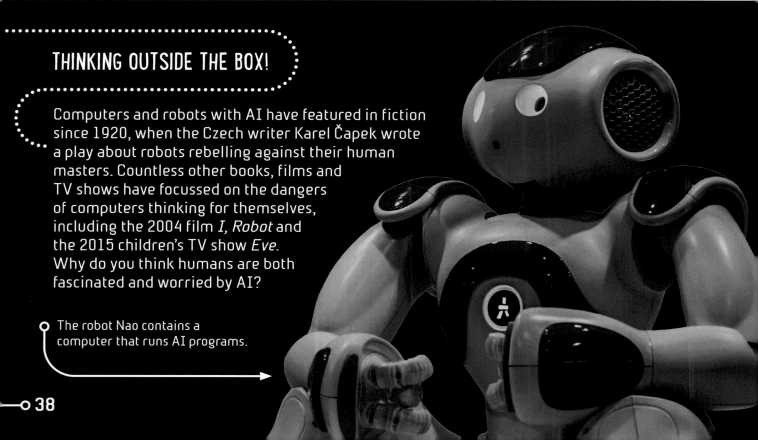

The robot Nao contains a computer that runs AI programs.

In 1950, Alan Turing (see page 23) developed a test to judge a computer's ability to think like a human. The Turing test has a human tester holding two 'conversations', one with a human and one with a computer, using a keyboard and screen so the tester cannot see 'who' they are talking with. The tester must judge which is the human and which the computer. In 2014, a computer called Eugene Goostman passed the test for the first time.

In the Turing test, a computer does not have to give correct answers, only the answers that a human would give.

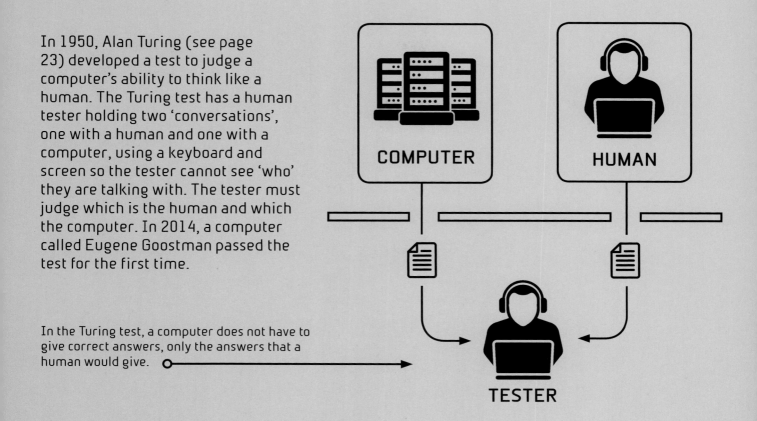

COMPUTER

HUMAN

TESTER

PROJECT

Intelligent personal assistants (IPAs) are programs that perform services for the user: for example, answering questions and booking restaurant tables using the web. Most IPAs use speech recognition and AI technology. IPAs decide between a range of answers and seem to get 'cleverer' at responding to their user by learning about their voice and habits. Some IPAs deliberately choose amusing answers to questions. If you have access to a personal assistant such as Apple's Siri, Amazon's Alexa or Microsoft's Cortana, carry out your own Turing test:

■ How many questions can you ask before the IPA gives an irrelevant answer?

■ What makes the IPA seem 'human'?

■ What makes the IPA seem like a program?

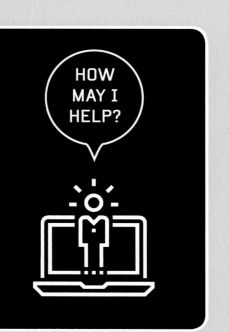

HOW MAY I HELP?

HALL OF FAME: AMAZING COMPUTERS

THESE EXTRAORDINARY COMPUTERS MIGHT CHANGE YOUR IDEAS ABOUT WHAT A COMPUTER IS AND WHAT WORK COMPUTERS CAN DO.

ALMA CORRELATOR

The ALMA correlator is a supercomputer at the ALMA (Atacama Large Millimeter/submillimeter Array) observatory, high in the Andes Mountains, in Chile. A supercomputer is a computer with many processors, not just one CPU. The ALMA correlator has 134 million processors and performs 17 quadrillion (that is 17 with 15 zeros!) operations per second. The processors combine and compare radio signals from space, received by the observatory's 50 radio antennae. The correlator enables the antennae to work together as a huge telescope, building up images of outer space.

RASPBERRY PI

This computer, which costs less than £25, is used for teaching computing in schools. It is sold as a circuit board containing a CPU and other basic hardware. It can be connected to an electricity supply, keyboard, computer screen and Wi-Fi networks. The Raspberry Pi has rows of pins, into which lights or other devices can be plugged. Students can learn to program the Raspberry Pi to make the lights turn on and off in patterns. Then they can move on to programming robots!

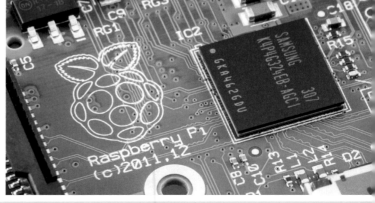

VOYAGER I

The space probe *Voyager I* is the furthest man-made object from Earth, which makes its three computers the furthest computers from Earth. *Voyager I* was launched in 1977 and passed out of the solar system in 2012. The three computers control the probe and its cameras. They receive commands from Earth and send data using the Deep Space Network. This network uses giant Earth-based radio antennae to transmit data.

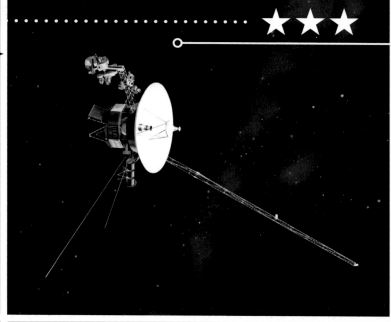

PACEMAKER

A pacemaker is a small electronic device that is placed inside the human chest to monitor and control heart problems. The machine uses electric pulses to keep the heart's muscles working normally. Pacemakers contain a computer, which can be programmed from outside the body by a heart specialist. These computers save hundreds of lives every day.

GOOGLE

Google is not just one computer but a network of around 900,000 powerful computers in Google's data centres. These computers allow the world's estimated 1.17 billion Google users to search the web using the Google search engine. Google can be seen as the world's largest computer, or computer cluster. A cluster is a group of connected computers that work together.

A CHANGED PLANET

SINCE THE MIDDLE OF THE 20TH CENTURY,
COMPUTERS HAVE CHANGED ALMOST EVERY
ASPECT OF OUR LIVES, FROM THE WAYS WE WORK
AND TRAVEL, TO THE WAYS WE HAVE FUN AND TALK TO EACH OTHER.

Before computers became common in offices, many typists and clerks were employed to type letters and documents on mechanical typewriters, or draw graphs and tables with pencils and paper. Before the first robot was put to work in a factory in 1961, factories employed millions of workers for manual tasks. Today, there are more than 1.6 million industrial robots. Although many people are glad to do less dull, repetitive work, others ask whether computers will one day put all humans out of work.

THINKING OUTSIDE THE BOX!

Workers no longer have to be in the workplace throughout the day. With email, workers can be anywhere with an Internet connection. Webcams allow meetings to take place without everyone being in the room. 'Telepresence' robots take this a step further. Using sensors, microphones and cameras, a worker who is far away can speak and see through a robot in the workplace, as if they are present. Telepresence robots are now used in education, for giving lessons in remote schools or teaching children who are in hospital.

The Internet has changed the way we interact with each other. The social networking website Facebook was launched in 2004 by Mark Zuckerberg and friends. By 2017, Facebook had 1.9 billion users, sharing their opinions, activities and photos. Today, some people may speak face to face with just one or two people a day, but 'speak' to hundreds or even thousands online. Although we may feel more connected than ever before, perhaps some of us are lonelier. Are our online 'friends' real friends? How can we tell if they are who they appear to be?

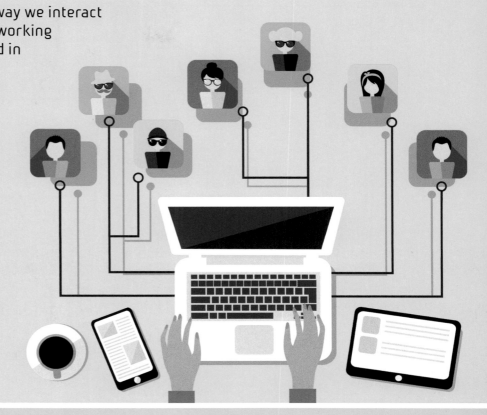

MATHS TALK

In 1950, there were just a handful of computers in the world. Today, around 350 million desktop and laptop computers are sold every year. In addition, at least 900 million smartphones are bought, as well as 200 million tablets.

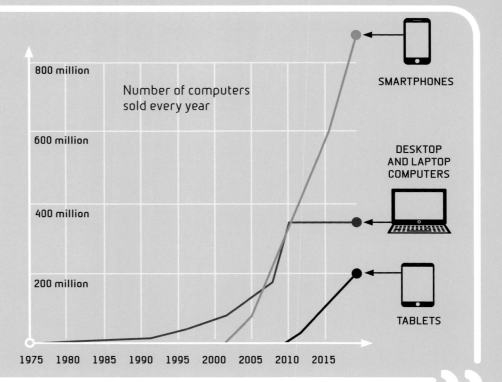

Number of computers sold every year

- 800 million
- 600 million
- 400 million
- 200 million

1975 1980 1985 1990 1995 2000 2005 2010 2015

SMARTPHONES

DESKTOP AND LAPTOP COMPUTERS

TABLETS

FUTURE COMPUTERS

SINCE THE FIRST ELECTRONIC DIGITAL COMPUTERS WERE BUILT 70 YEARS AGO, COMPUTERS HAVE BECOME MUCH SMALLER AND FASTER. HOW WILL COMPUTERS CHANGE IN THE NEXT 70 YEARS?

Computers will probably continue to get faster. However, many people think the current method of computing, using electrical circuits in chips of silicon, will have to be abandoned to make that happen. Ideas for new computing methods are being developed:

- **QUANTUM COMPUTERS** could use tiny natural particles to store and process data.

- **CHEMICAL COMPUTERS** could use mixtures of chemicals to perform calculations through their reactions with each other.

- **OPTICAL COMPUTERS** could use lights, which would turn on and off in a way similar to the electric currents in today's computers.

TECHNOLOGY TALK

Some of the devices in our homes hold tiny computers, which communicate with other devices using the Internet, creating the 'Internet of Things'. These connected devices are called 'smart'. We already have smart heating systems and smart kettles that are turned on using smartphones, and smart fridges that reorder food. In future, entire homes may be smart, with baths that run themselves at bathtime, and bedrooms that construct themselves at bedtime.

In the future, we may not use physical ('real') devices, such as laptops or smartphones. The 'devices' we use will be our own digital identity, unique to us, perhaps a name or number. Using that identity, we would access computing systems through non-physical portals (or 'doorways'), which have yet to be invented. Perhaps data would be viewed using a form of augmented reality.

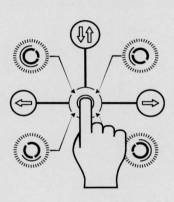

THINKING OUTSIDE THE BOX!

Another possible method of future computing involves integrated nano-electronics. 'Integrated' means 'linked in' and 'nano' means 'tiny'. This method of computing could work directly from our brain signals, which travel along our nerves as tiny electrical signals. When you wanted to use your computer, which might be worn or implanted in your skin, you would think 'switch on' rather than pressing the 'on' switch. This sounds like science fiction, but smartphones would have sounded just as far-fetched to someone living in the early 20th century.

GLOSSARY

algorithm A set of rules to follow when solving a problem.

animations Graphics that create the illusion of movement by showing slightly different images one after another.

artificial intelligence Computer programs that can perform tasks that usually require human intelligence.

binary With two parts; the binary number system uses only the digits 0 and 1.

central processing unit The 'brains' of a computer, where most operations take place.

circuit board A board on which electrical circuits are installed.

data Information.

database An organised collection of data stored on a computer.

data centre A building that holds many networked computers used for storing and processing large amounts of data.

digital Information or signals expressed as a pattern of 0s and 1s.

ebook A book that is read on a computer or other electronic device.

electrical circuits Loops around which electric current can travel.

files Collections of data that are stored as one unit.

hardware The machinery, wiring and other physical parts of a computer.

inputs Information fed into a computer.

Internet A worldwide network of computer networks.

joysticks Hand-held levers used to control movement in a computer game.

logos Symbols used by a company to identify their products.

microprocessors Small electronic devices that act as the 'brain' of modern computers.

motherboard A circuit board that holds the main parts of a computer.

networks Computers connected by cables, wires or wireless links.

pixels The smallest units of an image represented on screen.

processing Operating on data by passing it through a series of actions, using a program.

radio waves A form of energy used for sending invisible signals through the air.

RAM Random access memory; a hardware device where data is stored while the user is working.

ROM Read only memory; a hardware device that stores programs and data even when the computer is off.

search engine A program that searches for websites.

sensors Devices that detect and respond to light, sound or other physical properties.

social networking Using websites that allow people to connect with others.

software The programs used by a computer.

web A worldwide network of hypertext files, or 'websites', which are accessed using the Internet.

webcam A computer's video camera, which can send its images via the Internet.

wireless Communicating without connecting wires, usually with radio waves.

FURTHER READING

Digital Technology Tom Jackson (Franklin Watts, 2016)

Project Code Kevin Wood (Franklin Watts, 2017)

The Science of Computers Clive Gifford (Wayland, 2016)

WEBSITES

FIND OUT MORE ABOUT COMPUTERS AND PROGRAMMING AT THE FOLLOWING WEBSITES:

www.bbc.co.uk/education/topics/zs7s4wx

www.dkfindout.com/uk/computer-coding/

scratch.mit.edu/

QUIZ

- Express the number 21 as a binary number.

- Who invented the World Wide Web?

- Name an input device and an output device.

- What was the first feature film made completely with computer-generated

INDEX

QUIZ ANSWERS

- 10101
- Tim Berners-Lee
- Input devices include keyboards, mice, touchscreens and scanners, while output devices include screens, printers, speakers and lights.
- *Toy Story*
- The three computers on board the space probe *Voyager 1*

BUILDINGS

- Starting out ▪ Materials
- Structure ▪ Arches and domes
- Designing a building ▪ Scale and plans ▪ Perspective ▪ Ancient buildings ▪ Greeks and Romans
- Castles and cathedrals ▪ Architects
- Houses ▪ Eco-friendly buildings
- Skyscrapers ▪ Landmarks
- Public buildings ▪ Bridges
- Famous bridges ▪ Tunnels
- When things go wrong
- Hostile conditions

COMPUTERS

- A Computer is... ▪ Computers everywhere ▪ Ones and zeros
- A computer's brain ▪ Memory
- Inputs ▪ Outputs ▪ Programming
- Early days ▪ Computer scientists
- Software ▪ Graphics ▪ Games
- Personal computers ▪ Networks
- The web ▪ Virtual reality
- Artificial intelligence ▪ Amazing computers ▪ A changed planet
- Future computers

MATERIALS

- Choosing Materials ▪ Natural or Manmade ▪ Solid ▪ Liquid ▪ Gas
- Rocks and Minerals ▪ Wood
- Metal ▪ Glass ▪ Building
- Plastics ▪ Ceramics ▪ Textiles
- Art ▪ Composites ▪ Chemicals
- Super Materials ▪ Special Surfaces
- Shape Changers ▪ Recycling
- Future Materials

ROBOTS

- Designing a robot ▪ Moving parts
- Circuits ▪ Sensors ▪ Sight and navigation ▪ Code ▪ Programming robots ▪ Artificial intelligence
- Robot ethics ▪ The first robots
- Robots in danger ▪ Robots in space
- Drones and cars ▪ Real robots
- Household robots ▪ Robots and medicine ▪ Bionics ▪ Robotic arms
- Androids ▪ Fictional robots

SPACE

- Learning about space ▪ Our solar system ▪ Stars ▪ Galaxies and the universe ▪ Comets and meteors
- Black holes ▪ The Big Bang
- Astronomers ▪ Observatories and telescopes ▪ Space exploration
- The science of space ▪ Astronauts
- Training for space
- The International Space Station
- Space walks ▪ Rockets ▪ Rovers
- Space probes ▪ Satellites
- Space colonies ▪ Future exploration

VEHICLES

- Designing a vehicle ▪ Land vehicles ▪ Bicycles ▪ Cars
- Famous cars ▪ Trains ▪ Watercraft
- Boats and ships ▪ Hovercraft
- Aircraft ▪ Aeroplanes
- Helicopters ▪ Extreme terrain vehicles ▪ Power ▪ Materials
- Speed ▪ Braking ▪ Safety features
- Style ▪ Record breakers
- Vehicles of the future